T0169889

Sonnets
Salsa _and_

Other books by Carmen Tafolla include:

To Split a Human:
Mitos, Machos, y la Mujer Chicana

Sonnets to Human Beings
and Other Selected Works

La Isabela de Guadalupe y Otras Chucas

Curandera

Get Your Tortillas Together

Baby Coyote and the Old Woman /
El coyotito y la viejita

Sonnets and Salsa

Carmen Tafolla

Revised and Expanded Edition

Wings Press
San Antonio, Texas
2004

Sonnets and Salsa © 2001, Revised edition © 2004
by Carmen Tafolla.

First Edition, first printing 2001
Second printing, 2002
(original ISBN 0-930324-56-0)
Expanded, revised edition, 2004

ISBN: 0-916727-10-6

Wings Press
627 E. Guenther
San Antonio, Texas 78210
Phone/fax: (210) 271-7805
On-line catalogue and ordering: www.wingspress.com

This publication was made possible in part by a grant
from the Texas Commision on the Arts and the Texas Writers' League
and with the assistance of StoneMetal Press and Gallery.

Cover photograph by Bryce Milligan. Frontispiece and
author photographs by Rose Tafolla.

Library of Congress Cataloging-in-Publication data:

Tafolla, Carmen, 1951 -
Sonnets and Salsa: Revised and expanded Edition /
Carmen Tafolla
     p.   cm.
ISBN: 0-916727-10-6 (paperback)
(non acidic paper) Includes glossary.
1. Title. 2. Mexican American women – poetry.
4. Latina literature – poetry. 5. Texas – literature
2004
811'.54–TAF

*Except for fair use in reviews and/or
scholarly considerations, no portion of
this book may be reproduced without
the written permission of the editors.*

Dedicated to las comadres -
Antonia, quien lo inspiró,
Oralia, quien le dió alas,
y Dora, Velma, Sally, Rosie, Martha,
Barbara, Dorey, Carole y más, quienes,
con su fuerza y amistad, me han salvado la vida.

Acknowledgments

"Storykeeper," "La Gloria," "The Workers Who Build Our Nation," "'HealthCare' the sign says," "Fair," and "something" are previously unpublished. "La Isabela de Guadalupe y el Apache Mío Cid" first appeared in *Five Poets of Aztlán* (Bilingual Press, 1985) and is used with the permission of Bilingual Press. "La Malinche" first appeared in *Tejidos*, IV/4 (Spring 1977), and has appeared numerous times since, including in *To Split a Human Being: Mitos, Machos y La Mujer Chicana*, by Carmen Tafolla (San Antonio: Mexican American Cultural Center, 1985), in *Five Poets of Aztlán* (Bilingual Press, 1985), in *Infinite Divisions: An Anthology of Chicana Literature* (University of Arizona Press, 1993), and in *Sonnets to Human Beings & Other Selected Works* by Carmen Tafolla (Santa Monica: Lalo Press, 1992; reissued by McGraw-Hill, 1995; reissued by Wings Press, 1999). "Mercado" first appeared in *Sonnets to Human Beings* (see above). "Mujeres del Rebozo Rojo" first appeared in *¡Floricanto Sí! A Collection of Latina Poetry* (Penguin, 1998). "La Pasionaria" was first published as a broadside by Wings Press (July 1999), and subsequently by *La Voz de Esperanza* (Sept.1999). "¡Sí se puede!" was first published as a broadside by Wings Press (April 2003). "This River Here" first appeared in *The Texas Observer* (1996).

Contents

I. Selected Salsas

The Storykeeper	3
¡Sí se puede!	7
La Gloria	10
The Workers Who Build Our Nation	13
those things that were said to us	16
Mujeres del rebozo rojo	17
This river here	18
La Malinche	22
El Mercado	25
Farmer's Market (English version)	28
"HealthCare" the sign says	31
Fair	34
Fair (English Version)	36
something	38
La Pasionaria	40
La Isabela de Guadalupe y El Apache Mio Cid	44

II. Sonnets to Human Beings

Hot line	49
October 21st, 9 p.m.	51
Poquita allá	53
We never die	56
La Miss Low	57
La Miss Low (English translation)	60
Around us lie	63
La Querencia del toro	64
In memory of Richi	66
In Guatamala	68

Sweet Remember   69
Porfiria   74
Right in one language   78
Pedacito   82
Beyond our own   83
The magic   84
Living on the San Andreas   85
Statue of   86
The urge to write   87
Concha's brother   89
Chispa, the Pachuco sonnet   91
Come with me people   92
Nine moons dark   94
marked   97
They come from within us   98
Mission San José   100
Hay un lugar   101
Ancient workers   103
Gift design   104
Vision of a former life   105
No tienes límites   106
In love with people   107
How shall I tell you   109

Glossary   111

About the Author   115

I.

Selected Salsas

The Storykeeper:

instructions from an historian

In the *jarros*, she says,
Look in the *jarros*.
The ones forgotten or shoved aside,
with a broken clay lip and color dulled by years
of hard use
and unmeditated abuse.

Search between the folds of rags,
the places no one else would look.
Often they are there, hiding.

Look in the garage,
in the dark corners.
Sometimes they are undiscovered, silent,
in the *tecorucho* sheds out back
or dumped in the alley,
wiped away from our lives, for the trash to take.
Others, hoarded like treasures the holder fears to reveal,
wrapped in a homemade *colcha*, in a wooden box
under the bed.
In the *viejitos'* eyes, in the twilight of death,
you read their secret, the eyes point you to the spot, stamp
"Remember" on the almost-forgotten box, and plead with you
to be the keeper
of the story.
To open the box, unwrap the *colcha* carefully,
save the scrawled story
protect it
as best you can.

Look in the places where ink does not show.
In the breaking voice
between the lines of a song.
Our history
is written in that song,
written on the voice,
sometimes written
on the heart.

Look at the hands.
The way the woman crosses herself when she passes
a certain field.
Everyone knows the story
of what happened there
late that night ninety years ago.
Everyone knows,
but it is not written.
The paragraphs of dangling bodies were too long, too ugly
to be written.
The sentences, like unfinished lives, too short
to make sense.
The letters of the words, spelled out, distorted,
incomprehensible,
like mutilation of body parts
that started out in *belleza* and truth.

Look at the way she holds the masa, with both hands,
protecting, feeling its warmth,
memorizing the moment, for just a second,
before it's split apart,
into many *tortillas*
each to go their own way, some consumed rapidly,
some wasted, some disappeared,
never to be seen again.
In her gestures, her hesitations, her sigh of mourning,
lie our history.

Ask the whispers, she whispers,
breathed out in unguarded moments,
when the soul is too tired to think,
the body too worn down to hurt more,
in the numbness of the night,
when the father wrestles with the unwritten history,
pleading to save it, speak it, bury it,
staring at the pluma across the room,
avoiding the paper.
Singing the Indian chant of a story
he will not tell his children
yet:
'They are too young.
Only 10.
Or 16.
Or 36
Wait, Wait –
I fear for them to know
what those hate-filled others
did to my grandfather.
They are too young.
Perhaps I too at only 60
am too young
to know,
too old
to forget."

Ask the whispers, she chants, Learn the chant.
Sing it slow and privately
like he.
A sacred song
to be sung at only
sacred moments.

Look in the footwells of our steps,
the tablecorners rubbed smooth,

the marks on the walls where we have lived,
the fine and tired stitches in the clothing sewed and mended,
the careful fold of the shuck on the *tamal*,
the thumbprint curves of crepe paper flowers
trying to make '*Canta*' out of '*llores*'.
Learn to read the eyes, the hands, the spine.
You must be like a detective, or a spy.
Subtle, unnoticed, unrelenting.
For they are out there.
Our stories.
To be read in the tracks of tears now made
into wrinkles on the face,
in the scars we carry with pride,
in the grocery list marked with crayon on a junk mail
funeral home advertisement, in the Western Union
telegrams of money sent home to *México*,
in the eviction notices sent people whose address
has stayed the same for one hundred and fifty years.
You must be persistent, courageous. Go quickly. Urgently.
Go into the dark corners.
Unveil our treasures from the attic.
Go find it, hear it, touch it, write it down.

This is how
we keep
our
history.
This is how
we also
keep
our
soul.

¡Sí se puede!

a sixty-two-year-old woman,
her back permanently humped,
bending to strike with a short-handled hoe,
groaning in pain each time she bends,
the sun leaning hard on her aching waist

> (it was for *her* you spoke)

and for the fourteen-year-old boy
who leaves school every March and doesn't
return till November,
who can pick almost as fast
as his mother, but can't
add as fast as his Dad
(who had two years of school *en México*)
the fourteen-year-old who's proud
of looking sixteen
and has already started thinking
about how much money
he can add to the family budget after
he quits school

> (it was for *him* you spoke)

and for a six-year-old child fading
daily into cancer
("A very rare form among children,"
the doctor had shaken his head,
"except in this Valley, where we've seen
sixteen cases already this fall.")
whose Mother wonders whether
the child will ever get to see

the puppy she's requested
from Santa for Christmas,
as she looks out the torn screen window
and sees another red dragonfly
of a small plane fly low,
spraying the adjacent fields

(it was for *that child*
and that mother
that you spoke)

and the seventy-year-old man
who's worked in these fields
the last fifty-five years of his life,
but owns no papers to show
he has a right to stand on this ground . . .

and the nineteen-year-old girl
dreaming of study and college
and futures but knowing
it's no closer for her than a fairy tale . . .

and the young white businessman,
with a promising career, dying
of a disease that young girl
could have cured
had she been allowed
to get an education . . .

and the rest of us in the grey cities
and the purple mountains
and the steaming deserts,
and in the universities – still
learning to speak –
and the professions and the races
and the religions and

the genders still
trying to be heard,
the nations still struggling
to reach that oh-so-simple yet
oh-so-difficult
justice for all,
the factory workers and the doctors,
the sales clerks and the grocers,
the construction workers and the teachers
and all of us still trying to be human
and at peace . . .

       it was for *us* and for *them*,
          for *her* and for *him*,
             for *me* and for all
               those generations
                   yet to inherit . . .

it was for *us* you spoke and wrote and marched
and believed and prayed and fasted
                and died
for us . . . for all of us,
that You of the ready smile and the patient eyes,
the respectful ear and the gentle word,
with your insistence on non-violence
and your insistence on humanity,
that You, César Chávez,
lived.

Note: The first draft of "¡Sí se puede!" was read on April 24, 2003, at El Mercado, San Antonio, Texas, on the occasion of the unveiling of the U.S. postage stamp created in honor of César Chávez. A limited edition broadside of this poem was published on that date by Wings Press. A portion of the proceeds from the broadside benefit the United Farm Workers Union.

La Gloria

"Don't have much to show for it
but wha's mine is mine.
For whatever that means,
'cause none of it ever does show, anyway.
Not the real stuff.
Stuff on the outside don't count.
Todo eso can be taken away, ripped off,
messed up.
Or it gets old, wrinkled, faded.
But the stuff on the inside –
that's the stuff that gets better, stronger
not more worn out.
That's whas mine.
That's what I got.
Me.
La Gloria.

"Sounds stupid, eh?
Nobody thinks I got nothin.
Not even the good tips on the job.
(Well . . . 'cept once in a while.
And they don't get it why.
Young kids can't figure why
someone left me a ten dollar bill.
Once a twenty.)

"Ten long hours, sometimes twelve,
and then two buses to get home.
Then I just have time to pick up my kids,
check they done their homework,
make sure they ate supper
('cause that lady sometimes she just give'm
two spoons o' beenie-wienies!)

Bathe the little one
an' get'm all into pajamas.
Then they sleep an' I wash dishes,
wash the clothes or iron,
one or the other, every night,
and get to bed before the alarm goes off again
at five in the morning
and we start everything up again backwards from last night.

"Chure can't seem to get ahead
'cause it's always pay the doctor or pay the rent or
Sammy outgrew his shoes
or we're out of light bulbs or toilet paper.
And my back hurts but I can't stop
'cause tomorrow I gotta take off an hour to see the teacher
'cause Gina's having problems and she needs tutoring
or counseling
or something.
And I wish I had the money to buy a big picture of her
and put it in a frame on the wall.
But I just buy the wallet-size
and put it on a magnet on the refrigerator.

"Sometimes I think all I've got is the strength in my legs
or maybe my guts.
Or maybe whas living inside me.
But I keep on.

"*La Señora* that left me the twenty
she knew.
I could see it in her eyes.
She could see it in my face.
Saw the wince when I picked up the big tray
loaded down
and it hurt my shoulder

where I get that pain
Saw me call the babysitter on my break
whisper quiet "Mommy loves you."
Three times.
Saw me pick that tray back up and carry it out
with a smile.
Gracias a Dios que I got my legs.
They still working good an I'm forty-two!
Gracias a Dios que I got the other strong part too
inside, that thing that keeps me goin'
(don't know where
but goin')
Hardly no time to think about it anyway
'cept when I get on the first bus and sit
(second bus I'm figuring what I gotta do when I get home)

"Don't have much to show for it,
but whas mine is mine.

"And This is what it's like
to be livin'
in
La Gloria."

The Workers Who Build Our Nation

The workers who build our nation
run furtively
hide
have no right
to be here
only contribute
only donate
only build repair harvest plant hammer carry
babysit
raise our children
make our food
decorate
the tables with flowers and fine linen
at our most precious events
weddings graduations romantic evenings dinners in honor of
whisper
hide their faces
try to not be
apprehended
try to look
like they
belong

pick our potatoes
with their fingers
scraped raw by clods of dirt
gently pass our fruit
down from the tree
careful not to bruise
delicately served up on our plates
with all the freshness
of something innocent
something natural

Last night I dreamed
breathless, scared
jumping fences
climbing through razor wire
running in the dark
through thorny thick snake scorpion chaparral
through concrete crumbling construction barricades
and other people's pleasant-midnight-dream backyards
over fences, over hedges, over-under-run
that we
kept trying to escape
to be here
without being here
Illegal
just for being
Running
Staying
not allowed
Given no
right
to be
anywhere

And hoping, always hoping
not to be
found
out

I dreamed that when we finally reached
San Anto, home,
casa de mi tía,
casa de mis abuelos,
casa that belonged to me and mine
for centuries
we hid in the garage
hoping

not to be
found
out

morena, mojada, ilegal,
scared
the workers that build our nation

And then, I woke
whispering – a dream, a dream –
tried to convince, console myself

But I
knew
Saw the
news
the papers TV INS-trucks eyes
furtive looks by people
trying
not to be
too loud
too visible
too here

the workers who build our nation
pick and plant shovel lay concrete carry girders
beams bricks bushels bales trays babies
try
not
to be
too
much
alive

those things that were said to us

where go those things
that were said to us
and not heard
where go those words
that were almost whispered
from the thirsty tongue
cracked gray with crust of death
where go those messages
the mouth could not quite form
shaped around a groan
and we could not make out
but we saw the rolling eyes
and heard the tone
untold

where go those things
that were said to us?
In the morning,
the body is placed in the ground,
the flutter of the eyes
still echoing in my mind,
and by evening,
soft raindrops resting sentry,
the swallows have returned
home
to the earth-bricked mission.

Mujeres del rebozo rojo

Who are we,
las mujeres del rebozo rojo,
who are always waiting for the light
hungry for the pink drops of morning
on the night's sky
searching for the sparkle of creation, of beginning, of life,
on the dawn's edge
trying so hard
to open our eyes

Who are we,
las mujeres del rebozo rojo,
who want to reach and stretch and spread
and grow beyond our limits
yawning, pulling up our heads, pushing out our lungs,
arching out our arms
resting only when in growth, transition, transformation
wanting only to be, and to become . . .

. . . To unfold our lives as if they were a rebozo
      revealing its inner colors,
            the richness of its texture,
            the strength of its weave,
            the history of its making

Opening to
    all our fullness
    the blossom set free,
Spreading our wings to the reach of the sky
    and awakening
        to who
            we really
                are.

This river here

This river here
is full of me and mine.
This river here
is full of you and yours.

Right here
(or maybe a little farther down)
my great-grandmother washed the dirt
out of her family's clothes,
soaking them, scrubbing them,
bringing them up
clean.

Right here
(or maybe a little farther down)
my grampa washed the sins
out of his congregation's souls,
baptizing them, scrubbing them,
bringing them up
clean.

Right here
(or maybe a little farther down)
my great-great grandma froze with fear
as she glimpsed,
between the lean, dark trees,
a lean, dark Indian peering at her.
She ran home screaming, "*Ay, los Indios!*
A'i vienen los I-i-indios!!"
as he threw pebbles at her,
laughing.

'Til one day she got mad
and stayed
and threw pebbles
right back at him!

After they got married,
they built their house right here
(or maybe a little farther down.)

Right here,
my father gathered
mesquite beans and wild berries
working with a passion
during the depression.
His eager sweat poured off
and mixed so easily
with the water of this river here.

Right here,
my mother cried in silence,
so far from her home,
sitting with her one brown suitcase
and rolling tears of loneliness and longing
which mixed (again so easily)
with the currents of this river here.

Right here we'd pour out picnics,
and childhood's blood from
dirty scrapes on dirty knees,
and every generation's first-hand stories
of the weeping lady, La Llorona,
haunting the river every night,
crying *"Ayyy, mis hi-i-i-ijos!"* –
(It happened right here!)

The fear dripped off our skin
and the blood dripped off our scrapes
and they mixed with the river water,
right here.

Right here,
the stories and the stillness
of those gone before us
haunt us still,
now grown, our scrapes in different places,
the voices of those now dead
quieter,
but not too far away. . . .

Right here we were married,
you and I,
and the music filled the air,
danced in,
dipped in,
mixed in
with the river water.

    . . . dirt and sins,
    fear and anger,
    sweat and tears,
    love and music,
    blood.
    And memories. . . .

It was right here!

And right here we stand,
washing clean our memories,
baptizing our hearts,
gathering past and present,

dancing to the flow
we find
right here
or maybe –
a little farther
down.

La Malinche

Yo soy la Malinche

My people called me Malintzín Tepenal
The Spaniards called me Doña Marina

I came to be known as Malinche
        and Malinche came to mean traitor.

They called me – *chingada*
                        ¡Chingada!

(Ha – *¡Chingada!* Screwed!)

Of noble ancestry, for whatever that means, I was sold
into slavery by MY ROYAL FAMILY –
so that my brother could get my inheritance.

. . . And then the omens began – a god, a new civilization,
                        the downfall of our empire.

And you came.
        My dear Hernán Cortés, to share your "civilization"–
                        to play a god,

. . . and I began to *dream* . . .
        I *saw*,
                and I *acted!*

I saw our world
        And I saw yours
                And I saw –
                        another.

And *yes* – I helped you –
   (against Emperor Moctezuma Xocoyotzín himself!)

I became Interpreter, Advisor, and lover.
  They could not imagine me dealing on a level with you –
    co they said I was raped, used,
                      chingada
                          ¡*Chingada!*
But I saw our world
   and your world
    and another.
No one else could *see!*
          Beyond one world, none existed.
   And you yourself cried the night
   the city burned,
     and burned at your orders.
The most beautiful city on earth
           in flames.
You cried broken tears the night you saw your destruction.
My homeland ached within me
         (but I saw another!)

Another world –
   a world yet to be born.
And our child was born . . .
    and I was immortalized ¡*Chingada!*

Years later, you took away my child
(my sweet mestizo new world child)
    to raise him in your world.
   You still didn't see
      You *still* didn't see.
And history would call *me*
          chingada.

But *Chingada* I was not.
    Not tricked, not screwed, not traitor.
For I was not traitor to myself –
     I saw a dream
       and I reached it.
         Another world . . .

           La raza

              la raaaaaaaa-zaaaaa . . .

El Mercado

– ¡Molcajetes!
Listos pa' echarles su arrozito
pa' curarlos.
Velvet Pictures – pa' su sala, Señora –
Mira este tigre magnífico – o aquí –
Jesús, con su corona de espinas,
y el Presidente Kennedy
(que bueno era con los mexicanos)
pa' su comadre – la que anda muy
metida en eso de las neighborhood meetings!

"EXCUSE ME – DO YOU HAVE SOM-BRAY-ROES?
THOSE GREAT BIG ONES, YOU KNOW?"

¡Chiles! Frescos (y a buen precio.)
¡Chile petín! ¡Serranos! ¡Jalapeños!
¡Chile colorado ya molido!

"EXCUSE ME – ARE THESE HOT?

– It feels so hot already. Ya me anda!
My father used to call these days la canícula.

– Y la Tencha? ¿Porqué no 'stá hoy?
¿Se le falló el ride?
– ¿No oíste? iii – ¡qué tragedia!
Pos que su hermano – el que vive con ella –
se fue pa' la Social Security,
pa' que le pagaran lo de su retirement,
y que no le pueden dar nada porque su employer
no le había sacado pa' Social Security nada,
después de 40 años.

Y que le dolía el pecho
pero no quería ir con el doctor
porque decía que no tenía el conqué
y que todavía no llegaba al sixty-five
pa' Medicare –
y pos nomás se aguantó,
y ya no se quejó.

"IS IT FAR TO THE ALAMO?"

Y que ayer al regresar la Tencha a la casa,
con toda su montonota de florezotas de papel,
esas que vende ella y que les gustan
tanto a los gringos,
pos que al entrar a su casa,
cargada de todo y no viendo lo que estaba allí,
que se atropieza con el cuerpo de su hermano
en el piso, y se cae arriba dél,
con todo y flores.
Y el pobre – mas muerto que –
bueno, pos la Tencha que está
para matarse con pena que why didn't she
make him go to the doctor – y habérselo pagado
ella, aunque fuera a chorritos, como el lay-away.
Qué lástima, hombre.

– Si, pobre 'e la Tencha. Oyes, si pasas por su casa,
me traes las flores y lo que tenga a mercar,
y yo se los vendo aquí,
pa' que tenga la pobre
pa' sus gastos.

– Okay, 'mano. Y el helote
y la fruta que no se venda hoy,
se la llevo – al cabo que
mañana hay otro load.

– Sí, siempre llega otro load.
a-ay, así es la vida.
– Así es la vida.

– ¡Molcajetes!
Listos pa' echarles su arrozito
pa' curarlos.

Farmer's Market

(English Version)

– ¡Molcajetes!
All ready to be cured
with little grains of rice.
Velvet pictures!
For your living room, *Señora* –
Just look at this magnificent tiger, or here –
Jesús, with his crown of thorns,
and President Kennedy
(he was so good to us Mexicanos)
Get it for your comadre – the one that's so involved
in las neighborhood meetings!

"EXCUSE ME- DO YOU HAVE SOM-BRAY-ROES?
 THOSE GREAT BIG ROUND ONES, YOU KNOW?"

– ¡Chiles!
Fresh, hot, (and at a good price!)
¡Chile Petín! ¡Serranos! ¡Jalapeños!
¡Chile Colorado, all ground up already!

"EXCUSE ME - ARE THESE HOT?"

- It feels so hot already. It's bugging me.
My father used to call these days *La Canícula*, the Dog Days.

- And La Tencha? Why isn't she here today?
Did she miss her ride?

-Oh, you didn't hear? Eeeee – what a tragedy!
Well, it's that her brother – the one that lives with her –

went to the Social Security office
so he could get paid his retirement,
and that they can't pay him, they say, because his employer
hadn't taken out anything for Social Security,
after 40 years.
And that his chest is hurting him
but he doesn't want to go to the doctor
because he don't have the "with-what," you know?
And he's still not sixty-five
for Medicare –
so he just kept quiet and took it,
and didn't complain no more.

"IS IT FAR FROM HERE TO THE ALAMO?"

– And that yesterday, when Tencha gets home,
with that big ol' mountain of paper flowers in her arms,
the ones she sells, you know, and that the *gringos*
like so much,
well, on getting inside the door,
loaded down with everything and not seeing what was there,
that she stumbles on the body of her brother,
on the floor, and she falls on top of him,
flowers and all.
And the poor guy – deader'n a . . .
Well! That Tencha feels like dying of *pena*
que why didn't she
make him go to the doctor –
and pay it for him,
in little down payments or something,
like the lay-a-way at the stores *o algo*,
all feelin' bad, poor thing.
What a shame, hombre.

– Yeah, poor Tencha.
Listen, if you go by her house,

bring me the flowers and whatever she has to sell,
and I'll sell them for her here,
so the poor thing has for her expenses.
– Okay, 'mano. And the corn
and the fruit I don't sell today,
I'll take it to her –
after all que tomorrow is another load.

– Yeah, tomorrow is always another load.
A-ay, that's life.

– That's life.

– ¡Molcajetes!
All ready to be cured
with little grains of rice.

"HealthCare" the sign says

From where I sit
in a car on the highway back
from the border,
entering this city that flows
through my soul
like a river too dark and green to be anything
but just what it is,
The Taco Cabana sign
stands taller than the Tower of the Americas.

I'd tried to explain
to the tourist at the convention center
last week
how the river is ours,
our property, our deed and title,
personal wealth,
even though we sweat each month
to pay the rent
or be evicted
and sometimes
are.

But you cross the river and the underbrush
at city limits barely fifteen minutes from the city's center
and see nothing,
no sign of civilization's mark from the last two
or three
centuries
except for the very highway you are on.
And then, like San Antonio itself,
civilization surprises you,
appears full-grown and looking at you straight

with God's Eyes, honest, painful, asking questions,
as buildings meant to be
our epitome and strength
appear.

You blinked
or turned away,
dozed off a second
and here we are in the middle of downtown
still going way too crazy-highway-fast
past hospitals, hotels as high,
and office-building-shadows-trends gone by.

"HealthCare" the sign says
as I drive
but "No one cares"
unless you're wrapped in a green dollar bill
although the old part of the hospital still stands
and creaks and sighs
while arthritis attacks its legs.

The angel in the mural spreads her Vietnam Veteran wings
over a small child with a sick dove
despite protests to make her a Virgin,
especially in a Catholic hospital like this,
more cultural, traditional,
less prone to New Age healing fads, they recommend.

Off the highway now and we are here.
"Follow only new green highway signs"
the police officer tells us
"That way you'll get
where you are going."

We do not listen well.
That is how we have gotten
this far.

Orphaned by all the others,
we do not stand alone.

The river pays the rent for us.
We are her deed
and title.

Fair

Y que La Heather se sintió
porque la teacher dijo que
mi paper salió el mejor de la class,
el mas creative, el best expressed.

Y La Heather que always gets
the only "A plus" en English,
no había hecho perfect
esta vez
y piensa que es porqué yo le gané
a'drede para 'señarle
(después de ayer
que me burló por tener
vestidos comprados en Goodwill
y me gritó que "Mexican Face!"
Y que cara de medianoche
con dos lunas llenas.)

Y que se quejó con la teacher
que no era "fair."
¿Y que cómo era que alguien
que hablaba con acento
pudiera escribir un papel
de A Plus in English?
Y después le gritó a la mera maestra
que ELLA no era "fair."

Y después la teacher dijo
que todo el mundo tiene acento de algún tipo
que todo el mundo tiene algo que aprender
Y que "perfect" doesn't happen all the time.
Que la palabra "fair" tiene varios sentidos,

y que la próxima lección ese día
iba a ser de aprender
español.

¡Jiii-jo! Desde que llegó la "Bilingual 'Ducation" –
¡Que cambios, bro'! –
casi nos tratan como "equals" a veces.

Fair

(English version)

And that La Heather got upset
because la teacher said that
mi paper era el best de la class,
el most creative, y el best-expressed.

Y La Heather, who always gets the only A plus en English,
hadn't gotten a perfect grade this time.
An she thinks it's because I beat her
on purpose
to show her
(after yesterday
when she made fun of me for having
dresses from Goodwill
and called me "Mexican Face!"
y que Midnight Face
with Two Full Moons!)

And then she complained
con la teacher
que it wasn't "fair"
and that how was it that someone who
speak with an accent
could write a paper and get A plus in English?
And then she screamed a la mera teacher
that SHE wasn't fair!

Y then la teacher say
that everyone has some kind of accent
and that everyone has something to learn,
and that "perfect" doesn't happen all the time.
That the word "fair" has different meanings,

and that our next lesson that day
was going to be to learn
Spanish.

Jiiiiijo! Ever since we got La "Bilingual 'Ducation" –
What changes, bro!
Sometimes they almost treat us like equals a veces.

something

I look to you
keyboard
to say something to me
to bring me some intuitive wisdom
to console me, construct me,
converge me
to send me a message through my fingers
and your page
to reveal something
I wish I already knew.

I look to you
mailbox
to bring me something wonderful
to bring me something special
to change my life
to put something priceless
in my hands
that perhaps is already there
but I have no way of seeing.

I look to you
telephone
to transmit some important message to my ear
to give me news
good news
to make a connection
between me right here right now
and me someplace
in what I can be
and might become yet
but am still a stranger to.

I look to you
new day
perhaps tomorrow
perhaps tomorrow
always waiting for something
something
to happen.

La Pasionaria

para Emma Tenayuca
(December 21, 1916 - July 23, 1999)

La Pasionaria we called her,
bloom of passion,
because she was our passion,
because she was our corazón –
defendiendo a los pobres, speaking out
at a time when neither Mexicans nor
women were expected to speak out at all.

But there she was –
raising up her fist for justice,
raising up her voice for truth,
filled always with a passion
for life and for compassion,
a passion to empower the people
a passion to protect the poor.

A fire of heart and tongue.

So she raised her fist and her voice
'til the passion had spread like a firestorm
and the world was changed.

Such unflinching commitment to the truth
stirs fear and panic in some –
and love, in others,
empowered by that truth.

She was jailed and jailed and jailed again –
but that could not stop her passion.

A passion to empower the people.
A passion to protect the poor.

While pecan-shellers worked in dark halls
in clouds of brown dust that filled lungs
and brought a plague of tuberculosis,
while children missed school to work
twelve-hour days at rough-hewn tables
where no cool breeze or sunlight ever reached,
while people's fingers were bleeding
and their pockets were still empty,
and their children were still hungry . . .
she would not be silent.

Years later she would say to me,
"If I had had any hatred in those years,
I wouldn't have lasted at all.
Hatred is self-destructive . . .
you have to have Love for a cause."

No, Emma had no time for hatred,
no time for bitterness,
no time for regret.
She only had time for action,
for raising her fist and her voice,
for searching for the truth.

She read voraciously,
a one-woman university
a one-scholar library.

"Have you read Dostoyevsky?"
"Have you read Thorstein Veblen?"
"Have you read Barrera-Muñoz?"
"Have you read Sophocles?"
"Take this book."

"Take this book."
"Take this book."

Her black piercing eyes would educate us:

"I cannot go along with this extreme nationalism.
There IS a common goal for all of us – but it is not
isolationism, it is the right for human justice."

"The use of the Media to add superficiality
to the relationships between male and female
in America. . . ."

"Count the number of women in managerial positions
in our City Government. . . ."

"No ruling class can oppress another people without
some of the oppressed people within their structure
cooperating. SOME of us have accomodated ourselves
rather well. . . ."

"Have you looked at the position of women in Plato's
Republic?"

"Take this book."
Emma had a mind like a razor blade
but a heart that could fit
compassion for everyone –
even those who had no compassion for her.

Your mark was made, Emma,
but it wasn't made in stone,
it wasn't headlined in the books
that tried to erase your name from history.

Your mark was made,
but it wasn't pleasantly applauded on the naming
of streets and of public libraries
where the books you so loved were shelved
without noticing the heroine in our midst.

Your mark was made.
Your mark was made
on the course of history
y en el corazón del pueblo.

Your mark was made
on our lives,
on all of us
who are
still
following you.

Note: The first draft of "La Pasionara" was read at the funeral of Emma Tenayuca in San Fernando Cathedral on July 27, 1999. In 1938, at the age of 21, Emma Tenayuca organized 12,000 pecan shellers in a strike which boosted wages to five cents a pound. A powerful and courageous orator, she feared neither jail nor public censure. Her intellectual gifts were matched only by the greatness of her spirit.

La Isabela de Guadalupe y El Apache Mío Cid

I, as an India,
and you, as a Spaniard,
    how can we ever make love?

I, by mecate tied
  to a red dirt floor
  y una casucha de adobe
  en las montañas de cool morning
  and the damp of the wet swept floor.

Y tú, with your fine-worked chains
  tied from armor to iron post.
  White stallions, engraved gateways
  and a castle of hot night,
  fine tablecloth, chandelier etiquette,
  and pierce-eyed thoughts
  from the noble-blooded soul.
  Rey en España,
  Hacendado en México
  y Emplumado Emerador entre los Aztecas.

  Pero yo NUNCA FUI dese tipo!
  En España, gitana,
  en México, criada,
  y hasta entre Aztecas,
  yo no fui Azteca, sino obrera,
  cara triste,
  y calma.

I, que me gusta andar descalsa,
y tú, bordado en hilos de oro,
    how can we ever make love?

Will I have to crawl inside your armor?
Will you have to paint your feet with dirt?
Will we have to stop the world, take off its reins,
and tell it to go ver si puso la marrana?

Have you ever seen mecate elope with chains?

Will we have to meet between the day and night,
enlazados, esondidos, entejidos en amor,
with two masks and jet-way tickets labeled "Smith"?

Will we make a funny pair –
      red dirt floor and chandeliers?

Did we make that house already?
Did we already shift the worlds,
blend over blend in prism states,
moving between the mirrors of our many, many lives?

Dime ¿Am I really the criolla en manta?
      Are you really the apache in armor?
      Who did this for us already?
      Who gave my life to you to me to
         you and made it many-colored one?

I, as an India,
and you, as a Spaniard,
      how can we ever make love?

I, as an India and?
– You as campesino and?
– I as la reina and?
– You as indito and?
– Yo la azteca and?
– Tú el tolteca and?
– Yo la poblana y?

– Tú Mío Cid y?
– Yo la mora y?
– Tú el judío y?
– Nosotros la gente y
       nosotros
         la gente
           y . . . .
             Amamos.

II.

Sonnets to Human Beings

Hot line

(to my firstborn, firstdead; para m'ija)

The mark of you is soft and bright on my body
   The ridge is smooth up my belly
      disruptedly even
      deep and rich in color
                     and unforgettable

               like you.

The feel of it against my curious fingers
      is not like skin
      but different
         like promises and memories
         and passionate peace in one.

The scar is somehow like concentrated satin –
      a yard of it per half centimeter –
      rare, distinct, and full of voice and story
      (The aged *viejita* that I'd met
      so long ago had said
            "Each thing upon this earth
            has *voz, virtud, e idioma* –
            voice and use and language."

This mark of you on me
         is full
         of language

      and
         of
            love.

It is your gift to me.
Each night I can reach down and feel it,
listen,
hear your message

on this our own
     private

     red

     hot line.

October 21st, 9 p.m.
(autumn she don't waste no time!)

(to the autumn night sky)

. . . and the night gets sassy again
    and says "no way" she's gonna act hot and white
                    (or even hi yeller)

    when she's *really* feelin' cool and dark and slinky.

No way she's gonna dress up soft, light, sophisticated
                        and polite

    when she's really sharply naked, lustily growin'
    at the middle, and with every single
    freckle of a star
    showin' clear through
                  (– and no makeup to
boot!)

. . . she gets sassy,
        starts breathin' October-like –

           shivery and ripe,

      late harvest of a lady,
      no springtime gentle flower
      but one whose womb has swollen
      and whose heart has broken
      and whose spirit has picked up
      and moved on, and grown fuller,
                older,
        proud.

. . . the night, she gets sassy,
   ready to move up, or move on,
   but *move!* – no standin' still
   she don't keep life
   she swallows it
   gustily

   drops wiped off with a sleeve
   don't wait for table napkins
        – they come too late –
   Drink life n' laugh
   n' let it grow unreined
   let it be what it will be
                she says

. . . and her breezes pant strong
    she works hard
      plays hard
        breathes deep

           blows the useless stuff away –
              like leaves
                  from seasons
                        past
          looks to the root
          goes for the gut

          lays her earthy soul

          right up against her lover-man earth

              with nothin'

                in

              between 'm

Poquito allá

"This hand?
This hand?
It was an accident.
You do not understand –
Poquito aquí, poquito allá –
that's how Dios meant it, yes, to be.
It doesn't bother me too much.
In fact, it gives me less to work about.
Less people who will trust their broken chairs to me.
Yet I can still these roses plant,
like that one, standing by your feet –
'Las Siete Hermanas,' for they always bloom together,
like sweet sisters – seven in each bunch.
And I can still make *chocolate*, stirring strong,
the fingers do not slow me down –
these two, cut off, nor this one, sewed back on.

It's funny, don't you think,
how in those many years at Kelly Field
– or even in the war, *Dios solo sabe*, so many
around me dead, or legs or arms just floating off to sea –
but I came back (it must have been my mother's prayers)
the only thing the worse for it my teeth
(the Navy took us perfect, sent us back a mess.)
and yet –
I had so much –
aún every limb and digit there
my whole life full,
and so I can't complain.
This hand still does so much
for me – why just today
I planted ten small seeds –

cilantro for Mamá
(that woman loves it even in her beans) –
and pressed the earth down on them soft,
like her soft fingers when she caresses me,
and picked the eggs out for my sisters
y sus nietos – they taste different fresh,
like this – *las de las tiendas no comparan* –

But you want to know what happened?
Well, it's not too bad, *nomás que*
Chuy's neighbor still won't talk to me,
goes way around the grocery store
when he runs into me
I guess he's scared to see.
Some people, sometimes, *son así.*
Se siente mal, he feels bad, because he was the one who said
'Reach down in there for me and get that wrench'
and then he flipped the switch too soon –
ya casi era tiempo de salir –
I'd worked for him all day and he
was eager to pay up, clean up, go home,
and didn't wait to see that it was out.
Así – se acabó.
The doctors sewed this one back on,
aunque los que no están
molestan menos que éste aquí.

Too bad it bothers him so much.
I still do all I used to 'cept for
playing the guitar and carving wood.
The rest I do just fine, tho' maybe not as good.
Y el pobre, poor thing, always was uncomfortable
with Mexicans – *Y ahora peor,* he's worse.
Forgot to pay me for that day
or maybe scared to send the cash
for fear I'd ask for more.

Well, that's OK – this hand
still knows to *saludar*, shake hands, *y abrazar*
and only yesterday, my baby grandson stood right up,
solito, holding on to these good fingers
here.
Derecho, fuerte, unafraid.
Poquito aquí, poquito allá. . . ."

We never die

We never die.
We go through the trees in sunlight
hoping to be seen.
We never die.
We amass ourselves in sand dunes
awaiting patiently
the one who will record
our song.
We never die.
We take the wind's breath
and breathe it slowly
with all the living
with all those
who loved
Each in any way
The leaf bending to its branch,
The moon covering her earth asleep
with the warm worn coverlet
of her long black hair,
The unborn child dancing grateful
to the pulse
of its symphony-womb chamber,
And me,
drawn to the light in your eyes
that speaks colors of winter trees,
new-world skies,
dancing pearl-fetus, and sunrise
seen through the eyes
of the sand.

La Miss Low

La Miss Low era alta,
y delgada
y llevaba su pelo
pálido en su cabecita
como la cáscara
de un chícharo . . .
La Rosary siempre quiso
peinarla
bien pa' que se viera
bonita
pero como era maestra,
y nosotros chamacos,
no le dijo
nada.

La Miss Low se paraba
cerquita del Mr. Mason
pensando, creemos,
hacerse más elegante
al pararse cerca
de un hombre,
aún si era casado
y con su crewcut que soló
él pensaba le hacía verse mas galán.
Pero cuando él volteaba
la cabeza
pa' decirle unas palabras,
entre clases, en el corredor ruidoso,
eran nomás ellos,
ellos dos,
héroe y heroína,
entre todos nosotros

chamacos
y se sentía ella
grande
elegante
íntima
riéndose lentamente y formal de
cualquiera cosa
con él.

La Miss Low no hablaba mucho
trataba de levantar la cabeza
como figura noble,
de dejar a su silencio
(como guardián de la princesa)
hablar por ella,
cosas complicadas,
y muy sensibles,
de mantener la cara sin expresión,
mostrando así la nobleza de su alma,
de dar un ejemplo altivo
a estos niños incultos.
La Rosary decía que
peinándole el pelo
lleno y suave,
dejándolo crecer
un poquito más,
y poniéndole unos cuantos rizos
Pintándole la cara con más color
y enseñándole a guardar menos
sus emociones,
a mostrar más tranquilamente
su gracia natural,
que la podría
hacer
verse
más bonita.

La Miss Low era alta
y delgada
y posaba
como una estatua
de civilización
sin caos
mientras La Rosary
la veía
como tierra fértil, esperando semillas,
y Rosary allí, queriendo cultivar,
con cariño, su jardín.
"Did you get number 7?" le decía yo,
y abría ella su libro, con un suspiro largo,
diciendo, "Yo la podría hacer
verse
muy bonita."
Pero como era maestra,
y nosotros chamacos,
no le dijo
nada.

La Miss Low

(English translation)

La Miss Low was tall
and thin
and wore her short pale hair
tight around her small head
like the skin of a pea . . .
La Rosary always wanted to style
her hair
so she'd look
pretty
but since she was a teacher,
and we were just kids,
La Rosary told her
nothing.

La Miss Low would stand
close
to Mr. Mason,
thinking, we think,
to look more elegant
by standing next to a man,
even if he was
married
and with his crewcut that only he
thought made him look cool.
But when he turned his head
to talk to her
to address a few words to her,
between classes, in the noisy halls,
it was just them,
the two of them,
hero and heroine,

between all of us
kids
and she would feel
mature
elegant
intimate
laughing slowly and so politely
at anything
with him.

La Miss Low didn't talk much
tried to raise her chin
like a noble figure,
to let her Silence
(Guardian of the Princess)
speak for her,
speak complex, sensitive things,
to hold her face expressionless,
revealing the nobility of her soul,
to model a high example
for these
uncultured children.

La Rosary said
that by styling her hair
full and soft
letting it grow a little longer,
putting in a few curls,
putting more color in her make-up,
teaching her to let herself go,
to be more natural,
that she could make her look
prettier.

La Miss Low was tall
and thin

and stood
like a statue
of civilization
amid chaos
while La Rosary
saw her
like fertile ground,
awaiting the planting,
with Rosary
wanting to cultivate
with tender care, her garden.

"Did you get number 7?" I'd ask her,
and she would open her book, with a long sigh,
saying "I could make her look
really pretty."
But since she was a teacher
and we were just kids,
La Rosary told her
nothing.

Around us lie

Around us lie
the messages
babes born voiceless
hearts whose vaults
do not know
how to seal
linked helplessly
to our machines
carrying quiet
the blue eyes that were
requested
while the sun-skinned throngs
fight to eat
and hear no requests
from anyone
The machines laugh smilelessly
they would ask of us
epics
in elaborate colors
but we hum
drumbeats
while carving clean paper
with pens that write
in black ink
only

La Querencia del toro

to George and María

– Picked and angered, bleeding from the banderillas
wagging on him still in irritating flashes of sharp ribbon,
taunted by the smell and roar of fear and anxious urging,
the bull reaches his querencía, this little holy high ground
he will stand and not leave, until he wins, or dies.

By four every day the old man is at the park,
limps garbage can to garbage can
takes the empty Coke cans out,
stomps them with his good foot
and stores them in the bag.
The old nun chants "I am not worthy. I am not worthy.
I am not worthy." to her soul,
face blank, from practice.
At four in the morning the middle-aged Chicano
too young, too brown, too smart,
can't sleep from the news, the one
curt page of pretentious evaluation
from a nervous boss whose work he'd done too often,
climbs up Marshall Peak, puffing anger out
and disappointment
meets the *tecolote* – owl
with wingspan wider than his own
and racing down the hill, survives,
his spirit healed by places
where defeat is honest.

The old white house with gingerbread
trim is torn down by the city
And so the tiny aqua one, built on the half-lot
all the way to the back.

A two-year-old girl, crying angry pride
that Discovery is Punished,
steals the kitchen knife quietly
and builds houses of moist mud
under the house.
These may stay
for quite a while
until the owl's children
have landed
quietly
on blank-labeled cans.

In memory of Richi

First day
of school
for both of you
– one of you six and glowing copper,
    running with eagerness and proud
the other 22, young pale teacher,
    eager for this school

Your blue eyes warm to his brown stars
as you both chat
and share your missions,
as you ask his name.
He rolls it like a round of wealth
and deep in Spanish tones, responds
        "Richi."
You try to imitate, say
        "Ritchie."
"No!" he teases, confident,
"It's Ri-chi – just like this."
You notice that each syllable
could rhyme with see
and try again.
He pats you on the back.
You go on to your separate tasks –
he to his room, you to yours.

One day, six hours,
really not a speck of sand
in all this shore of time, and yet,
so crucial,
as you gather papers,
turn to flee the cell

and gain some comfort
in some other place.
Your ray of hope
comes filtering down the hall.
In eagerness for someone's warmth,
you shout and wave,
     "Hey, Richi!"
He corrects,
the light and wealth all gone
from his new eyes,
     "No.
       Ritchie."

In Guatemala

there are no political prisoners
only men's heads that show up sewed
into the now-pregnant bellies
of their fiancé's corpses

only hands that open
from the jungle floor,
fingers crying "*¡Justicia!*"
as they reach like vines trying
to break free

only butchered organs
pressed into the earth
beneath the feet
of "government" officers

only Ixil Indians in rebellion,
their red woven messages of humanness
in whole Indian villages corraled, beheaded,
for existing too full
of straight-backed dignity

There are no political prisoners
There are no *problemas de derechos humanos*
There are no repressions in free democracies
There are only Presidents
who scratch each other's backs,
blindfold each other's eyes,
laugh uncomfortably,
puffing the finest
popular-name cigars
and cutting too-human heads
from the non-human bodies
of non-justice.

Sweet Remember

Sweet Remember
when you ask your little girls to be
so sweet,
sit neat,
cry easy,
and be oh so pretty on a shelf

When our young women
who are decent
are to always be
in company
of strong young men
who can
protect them

When girls and women
are expected
to play at home,
which others should protect,
to always breathe in innocence
and seek a shield from heavy news and death,
to sing and paint
and, when appropriate,
to scream and faint

Sweet Remember
that Marta Diaz de C.
had her legs spread
on an electric bed
as someone probed
with great delight
to see her scream
'til dead.

Sweet Remember
that Cristina R.L.G.
was taken in the night
from her parents' home
and husband's bed
and forced to talk
with massive rape,
incontinence, indecency,
and forced to faint while
hanging by her knees
wrists tied to feet, 'til circulation ceased.

Sweet Remember
Elsa B.
whose naked 3-year daughter
was immersed
in ice-cold water,
as the Sergeant pulled her tits and whispered in her ear,
"Whore, come sleep with me
and do it sweetly
or we will not let
the child's head up
until she kicks no more."
And when she did,
they threatened a
Portrait in Two:
Whore and Child Whore –
side by side in bed
with plenty volunteers
to tear them both
right through the core
mass party rape in
stereo
and screams
galore

"and then we'll know
where we can find
and kill
your husband."
And sad and sick,
to save her child,
she spoke.

And Sweet Remember
young Anita S.
who was raised to think her womanhood
was in her breasts
and inside panties and to be covered
in a dress
and then,
because the village teacher was
a critic
of the government,
and a family friend,
she was "detained,"
and called a Marxist,
had her breasts
slashed at with knives
and bit by soldiers eager
for their flesh
and had then "Communist"
burnt with electric pen
and shocks
into her upper thigh
and her vagina
run by mice,
and lived to know
her womanhood
was in her soul.

and Tina V., María J., Encarnación,
Viola N., Jesusa I., and Asunción
who screamed first and did not think to strike
who'd never fired a gun or learned to fight
who lost their husbands, parents, children, and own lives
and oft'times dignity or body parts or eyes
and some whose pregnant nipples tied with string
were yanked toward opposing walls
and back
till babes were lost
and blood was running black.

Sweet Remember
this is why
I do not ask
my child to cry
to sit sweet helpless and be cute
to always need a male escort
to think that only he protects,
not she, herself, and not she, him
to think herself so delicate
so weak,
to hold as inborn right a man's protection
or his pity for a tear on pretty cheek

But I will teach her
quite instead
that she is her own brave life
till dead
and that there are no guarantees in life
nor rights
but those that we invent
and that the bravest thing of all
to think, to feel, to care, and to recall
is to be human
and to be complete

and face life straight
and stand on solid feet
and feel respect for her own being
temple, soul, and head
and
that she owns her strong brave life
till dead

Note: All of the incidents of torture mentioned in this poem were document-ed by Amnesty International. Only the names have been changed.

Porfiria

Porfiria doesn't exist
but if she did
she'd say "¡Que se chingue Reagan!"
          "¡Rómpenles el borlote!"
          y "Tráigame una cerveza, Carlos."

Porfiria liked Carlos –
liked the way he'd take
his pocket knife out,
in front of white liberal gringos
and clean his fingernails with it,
tryin' to look mean,
tryin' to look like the image of Mexicans they were
trying hard to unbelieve.
Porfiria'd say,
not too committed to any one view,
          "Chale, you're okay."

Porfiria didn't like people who were
so committed to the truth
they couldn't see anything else.
But Porfiria wasn't prejudiced –
she didn't like people neither
who were scared of coming down hard
and being violently close-minded –
saying, like those wonderful, crazy intellectuals
visiting from Latinoamérica would say,
"¡Está usted loco!
¡Cómo puede creer tal cosa!
¡Está completamente equivocado!
¡Es una tontería increíble!"
She liked that.

Took guts to say it like that,
'steada conference talk, a la USA,
"The distinguished Dr. Satdunk
certainly has a profound comprehension
of the field, but he seems to be forgetting
one major factor, which could disprove
his entire . . . pardoning my boldness, but . . ."
Porfiria said that was
                    "Chicken shit! Big Mask
                    to hide Little Heart!"
or the way she put it
when she was feelin' good:
                    "Paper Prick to hide Bubblegum Huevos."

Porfiria doesn't really exist
but if she did
she'd be the kind to say "Ya Basta,"
put a sig-gar in her mouth,
like Generala Carmen Robles,
1915 Special, Field General, Mexico-style,
with her men and women standing by her
and say quiet, with the smoke blowin' out slow
every word heavy and dead-eyed
                    "Ya ha comenza'o
                    la revolución"
and her dead eyes nail you, dying,
with that unspoken final curse word
meanin' "you."

She'd be the kind to get upset about
the uptight, lowdown two-headed academics –
one head playing Brown Beret and
dressing ethnic on the Diez y Seis
(Veevuh luh Rozz-uh, Man!)
other playing bouncing puppy dog

(Yes boss! Yes boss!)
can be bought for less than money –
title, publication,
mention in the Central Office Minutes . . .
        "Oh, shit!" she'd say,
        then turn and put a crazy GI hat
        on and drink beer to German music
        all night long.

Porfiria'd go home   tired
apologize to her cat
for not putting the food out on time
        say, "Chinga'as d'esas fregaderas.
        Ni me dejan tiempo de prender la vela."

        "Y ustedes – ¿que?"
        responds to puppies scrapping,
        nicknamed Gringo and Chicano,
        "A lo menos pueden aprender
        a no cagar en casa ajena."
        strokes their necks and
        turns to light the vela
        that spiritwarms the house and
        catches lightdance off a tear
        as "Firia" mends her mother's colcha for her,
        thinking.

        Porfiria sat on a few committees
        was quiet a lot
        occasionally mumbled
        and once in a while let loose an'
                "¿Y qué pendejos porqué no?"
                or even worse a just plain, "Why?"
        Got criticized for "lack of finesse"
        and answered, for the soflameros,

"I handle too much shit
to use a dust rag and
furniture polish on it.
Shovels work just fine."

Porfiria doesn't exist,
in the usual way
    has no photograph,
    social security number,
    or signature.
But Porfiria has just so damn much to say
that she will show up anyway, stubborn bitch,
that we will
      everyone of us
       take a picture
        invent a number
         sign a declaration
              for her
        even if it has to be
        with our very own
        names.

Right in one language

"Write in one language," they say
and agents sit and glare hairy brows
over foreign words, and almost trying hope,
say, "It's not French, is it?"

But it isn't.

Nor is my mind
when I try tight, clean line
manicured to be like Leave
it to Beaver's house
                straight sidewalk
                so square hedges
                and if there's one on
this   side there's also one on   that
Equally paced
        placed
        spaced
        controlled

"You seem to lose control of the line
in this one," he says, "it all explodes."
        I see bilingüe-beautiful
            explosions –
                two worlds collide
                two tongues dance
                    inside the cheek
                    together
Por aquí, poquito   and a dash allá también
    salsa – chacha – disco polka
Rock that Texan cumbia
in a molcajete mezcla!

But restrain yourself –
the Man pleads sanity –
Trim the excess –
just enough and nothing more
Think Shaker room and lots of light –
two windows, Puritan-clean floor, and chairs
up on clean simple pegs – three –
y
   las
      palabritas
         mías
              are straining at the yoke

two-headed sunflowers
   peeking through St. Moderatius grass
      waiting for familias grandes
garden growing wild
   with Mexican hierbitas, spices, rosas,
      baby trees nurtured así, muy natural
      – no one knows yet
      if they're two years old
      and should be weaned
              or pruned
                  or toilet trained
      but they are given only
      agua y cariñitos,
      shade and sun and compañía
City Inspection Crew,
House and Gardens Crew,
Publications Crew agree
the lack of discipline
lack of Puritan
purity
pior y tí.

Chaucer must have felt like this,
   the old Pachuco playing his TexMex onto the page
and even then the critics said,
     "Write
        in one language."
But he looked at all that cleanness, so controlled,
   forms halved, and just could not deny
his own familia, primos from both sides,
          weeds that liked to crawl
          over sidewalks, pa' juntarse,
          visit, stretch out comfy,
          natural and lusty
          hybrid wealth,
and told them it was just because
he was undisciplined
     unpolished
        and did not know
           how to make love
           with just
           one
           person
           in the room
           or
           on the page

And he, like me,
did what he wanted anyway
But
You, like they,
want Shaker hallways
and I grow Mexican gardens and backyards.
There are 2 many colors in the marketplace
to play modest, when Mexico and
Gloria Rodríguez say,
"¡Estos gringos con su Match-Match,
y a mí me gusta Mix-Mix!"

There are 2 many cariños to be
      created
to stay within the lines,
2 many times
when I want to tell you:
      There is room
        here
       for two
      tongues
     inside this
       kiss.

Pedacito

When long it takes to craft with care
This miracle of skin and soul and breath,
And blessingworth we find the pain to bear,
Say, *"Pedacito de la luna, usted,"*
Give light, give love, protect and fuse to heart,
But then the homage pay to death,
See precious life grow tall and march to war,
Immune to wonder then, we halt the breath.

Chest still, moon cold, we distance from the heart.
Forgetting we are linked to light,
The human loses, but we win the war.
What then the goal? Why cannot we respect
To see in life's form fully grown,
Say, *"¿Pedacito de mi corazón?"*

Beyond our own

Heeding the call of a mockingbird
whose voice has crackled with the plight
of unknown days and loveless nights
and human voices left unlearned,
it is but time that we have left
to bargain with in measured bits
and say to him, "We know the plea,
but have no answer ready yet,
no face with which to give us sight,
no heart of which to give our face."
We are inferior to your heed,
for we have yet to hear the voices –
even one beyond our own.
Not even one beyond our own.

The magic

to the child in the photo (and all the others)

Such magic in a child there is, such life,
Such fountainburst of days and love and hope,
The magic breath of tiny hands and heart
That beat and breathe and suffer, try and cope.
But ribs, like tree roots arching to the skies,
Face upward, caking o'er the ground so dry,
And hunger curls the spine, affronts our eyes:
You will not live. And yet, you will not die.

The love that ripened in your first wet cry,
The hope that sheltered you when arms could not
Will not retreat nor silent keep their sigh:
In naked truth they lash our superficial lies
          (like war and wealth and coldness comfort-taught.)
Your eyes now frozen in the lens and paper flat
          give hope that our hearts cold might yet survive.
For this, you will not know but grace, and, dove,
In truth as death, you will not be but love.

Living on the San Andreas

Wondering if Nostradamus meant us . . .
Wondering if the California Indians' claim
the air made us crazy was . . .
Wondering if the smog has done that already
Wondering why there are so few poets
in this town
or if blindness will bring sanity
wondering why I pull my hair out
by the roots
criticizing the ends
Wondering why we are straddling this
daily,
babes in our arms,
Wondering what
we are doing
here.

Statue of

Statue of
Teeming hordes of hungry
Always wanting just a
Time of rest not waiting
Under suffocated souls
Even scared to breathe too loud

Or ask
Freedom from the

MIGRA who will hunt them down

The urge to write

The urge to write
to squeeze your child until she breathes
The urge to write
to take the cut head down from the tree

The urge to rain dance, rain dance
pour the teardrops on the tongues
cool the fevers
hock for grain the guns
Pour the sweat from spas
onto the dying fields
Take the steam from worry greed
into village kitchens, warm the frozen bodies
give them meals

Sundance kiss the stiffened lids of corpses
open eyes from death and hate
pump the hearts with open palms
bow to nature breath and reins

The urge to sieve the rivers
                              red with blood
return the hearts to lovers praying
To rebuild, clay by clay, with sun,
with water, food, and touch, the human form
To peel off finecloth uniforms
and turn them to the bandage
To touch the skin until it shivers warm

The urge to take the huddled bodies
out of tunnels, trunks – Beknight
with life and freedom

and with right

The urge to
Breathe

The urge to shout
Do not die
    alone

Concha's brother

Concha's brother
beat his first wife
(and said he loved her still today)
always got drunk for funerals
and tried to ready-start a fight
with any *gringo*, especially a cop,
sometimes cheated people who came to his garage
always got angry at anyone waiting on him
and liked to say, "Where there's smoke, there's fire."

Concha's brother
wrote all the bad checks,
got all the girls pregnant,
crossed all the lights late,
and even stole a fifty dollar book for me once,
and gave it to me, *con mucho respeto.*

Concha's brother
made the best *fajitas,*
barbecued like a reigning king,
and did it in the front yard, inviting everyone,
especially on special occasions,
like the birthday of his daughter,
(daggerdeep dimples like he,
and laughing)
telling jokes like only he could,
adding extra spice to everything
and everyone drinking
all they could.

Concha's brother
divorced his second wife,

remembered neat times with the first,
said again he loved her still
and always played pool with
her brothers.

Concha's brother
cried late at night
all alone
and the tears mixed
with the beer
and the sweat
and the loneliness,
and the only things
that brought
the sun
up
for another day
were his daughter,
the jokes he told so good,
and those barbecued *fajitas*
he did in the front yard
inviting
everyone

Chispa, the Pachuco sonnet

When stubborn Chispa takes cowhead and tripe,
And makes of it a feast that thirty years
Will turn into expensive fare and ripe
To whims elite from poverty's arrears,
And ese vato glides, his pose the deer's,
But head held back at angle to the sun.
The slant of pyramids his body hears.
The Aztec thus danced too, same angle done.
Another's gesture comes from Babylon.
The word from Africa transforms, survives.
The song of China lingers on the tongue.
Posed also to the sun, Quetzalcoatl smiles.
Chispaseed, the spirit never dies, the flame
of centuries' sabor is carried on, the same.

Come with me, people

Come with me, people
Let me feel the soft breeze
smiling closed eyes
with cuddled love.

Come with me people
Let me feel your blood slow
with the morning sun
and your heart beat plain
like the country axe at its daily wood.

Come with me people
Let me feel your breath drawn in
deep and long and drinking full
the scent and feel and warmth
of human breath around you,
used and re-used like a kitchen tool
passed from one to next to next,
gaining flavor and smooth edges.

Come with me people
Come with me now
and let us leave behind
those tiny orbs of shining steel
where people keep themselves
so safe
so separate
and
so all alone.

Come with me people
Let me come with you
to where air and sun
and living spirits
blend together
gently.

To where air
and sun and
living
spirits
blend
together
gently.

Nine moons dark

– This is what it takes to make a child –

Nine new moons of dark hot wind
and careful mouthfuls, hoarded, pointed,
sent direct to fill the small one,
Empty *jarros*, *ollas*, make the magic prayer,
and corn tortillas carry forth alone
the gifts of all.

Grace from spiritdancers gives the balance
over holes and rocks
that make the street,
to keep the swollen womb
from falls and blows.

One treasure-bought
small handmade *vela*,
lit in prayers to
Indian Pregnant Virgin,
still in name the goddess free
pre-fires and pre-cross
Guadalupe
Tonantzín.

And last a blessing
from the eldest face of corn
Hand, even warmer, gives the
touch, the shape
of welcome.

Past the rabid dogs
the knifecold brows

the hungry pouts
searching for purse –
there is none.
Past the street lights' angry metal blare.
Past the profit eyes
that buy the babes
before their birth,
grabbing,
appetize a bill for 50, 20, any
strange-faced tender
under trembling fingers
of the ones whose other
children starve at home
and some, caught between
foodsilence and
fullarmscrying,
follow, into
a car.

Past the doors of public *Hospital Civil*,
pulling her *rebozo* tighter
round her dropping belly, rising life,
her tiny claim intact.
Nineteen years seems
long enough to wait
for this small cry,
the very first,
Feels the head emerging
strong

the tiny heart pounds out
its shout of proud Survival

small investment, kicking
whisked away
passed hand to hand

changed arms to arms to beds
and on the road, new papers, forms
a neat 10,000 chopped
in many stops and stages
To Northern Nursery's Lie:
Money buys it
all.

And somewhere at the *Hospital Civil,*
A scream undying burns:
This one's not mine!
This dead one pulled from your icy *hielera*
for the cool fleshmarket's use
The scream goes on, unchanging, strong,
as if to heat their hells
and rip their walls
and reach the wind, to touch
that one of hers,
so far.

Nine new moons of Indian-color-earth enfolding
warm as blood and turquoise-feathered prayers
and all they give her
is that purpled baby, cold,
refrigerated, preserved,
thrice-abandoned, reused
to move their market

that baby
cold
touched soft at last
by her pain-partner fingers
whom even her
long burning scream
of rage and love
cannot warm.

marked

Never write with pencil,
m'ija.
It is for those
who would
erase.
Make your mark proud
 and open,
Brave,
  beauty folded into
 its imperfection,
Like a piece of turquoise
 marked.

Never write
with pencil,
m'ija.
Write with ink
 or mud,
or berries grown in
gardens never owned,
 or, sometimes,
 if necessary,
  blood.

They come from within us

They come from within us
those unwhispered spiritchildren of our souls,
from within the fifth womb of us
unbirthed spiritchildren,
conceived and then dissolved,
absorbed into us

You will see them
everytime I dance forgotten swirls
You will hear them
in the quiet eeking half-screams
        in the night
You will know them
in those strange glances
that lightning from my eyes
        but do not
        belong to me

They come from within us
spiritchildren that
bloomed in
tiny half-buds
deep in our untainted hideaways
in the fifth womb
of the fifth soul
where their spirits rested
long enough
to give their presence
to us
and then disappear,
goodby-whisper unannounced,
blend into our blood,

kiss the holy quiet spots
and leave,
the spirit tracks still in us

They come from within us
When you hear me
instead of them
it is by chance
for they come soft and silent,
resting only
between
missions
and
within us.

Mission San José

The rocks are warm
have had the hands upon them
through the years
with sun to bake in
memories.
Gentle, even with
ungentle missions,
somehow life got through
to them,
the priests amazed
that rabbit tasted
good,
slowed their passion fervor
one San Antonio sunny afternoon
learned to
lope
a bit
and breathe
with warm brown human flesh
touched the rocks in
tenderness
one time too many,
ceased to call it mission
as it grew to make itself
home
for all of us.

hay un lugar

Hay un lugar
There is a place
where corn is ground by daily arms
and old metate smoothed by flow of family
to make tamales where the kernels
keep their character
and wealth

There is a place
where supper tables feel the pulse of human hands
and breathe it back to them, with blessings,
respecting life and death and age, each in the other,
thing of flesh to thing of wood,
with boundaries forgotten

There is a place
where the stone comal warms gifts
from gardens that are asked,
and each plate is prepared
and carved to fit the tastes
for that one mouth
whose sounds are known so well
and warmth is added from the hands that love

There is a place
where early morn adobe walls
retain the day's high sun
and spread its warmth so kindly
through the night

There is a place where hands grow old,
the wrinkles kept intact and kissed,

a place where babies still get bounced
to dancing-song of whisper:
"all the world's your own"
where eyes lift up in gratitude to sky, and
even zopilotes have a softness to their name

There is a place
hay un lugar
donde hay un lugar para tí

Ancient workers

the hand

shows lines

engraved

by ancient workers

each in line

chipped out its mark

to write the letter

say

we are all here

together

in you

Gift design

made for an older human

Turquoise speaks the fire

and the soul.

White shells, the Peace.

Brown twigs,

children of the grasses,

the evidence of imperfection,

highest compliment.

Vision of a former life

Breathe
shallow
Breathe
like sand in sunlight
poised silent

A dog crosses
the Pueblo afternoon,
absorbs the shadows

To arrange
the painting in the sand
(my work)
    I do not place
    the pieces
    I breathe
    with them,
    lightly

No tienes limites

a slice of you
does not fit on paper
                    (unless one wears
                     glasses ground with filters
                     for the sun)

a slice of you
bursts with pleasure
in the mouth
can only be tasted
at midnight
when ink cannot testify
and time and conciousness
are turned off
so humans can exist
without limitations

In love with people

It occurs to me that we
are all in love with people.
We see the plump-pout lower lip,
the smoothness of a temple scar,
the eye that flickers between words
and, on them, shrouds in cinders.
We lie in wait to see them pass
and drink up, as they talk.
I stare at this one with wide hips
and full moon eyes – the weight looks good
it settles soft, relaxed, no laws,
And that one there, my *primo*,
just a little bit *loquito*,
eyes a little crossed, wire glasses little
out-of-style, smile a little sweet,
frame a little tall and bent.
The ten-year-old *pachuco*-child
trying so hard to be so cool,
shows me the way to "pop,"
the way to "break," then shyly states
"I do it better than this
sometimes."
It occurs to me that we
are all in love with people.
The way the strands soft-frame the face
or teeth jut out so brave and out of place
but innocent; on this one here the nose
turns pointed down, suspiciously;
on this one apple cheek crowds cozy
up against white lashes cuddling.
The way that wee hand clings,
its dimples hugging wrinkles;

that smile so full of metal teeth;
that face so dark that it absorbs;
the way the thousand craters on this face
are like a lava field, complex and rare,
or other things that catch us
loving people – how your eyes
stop like culprits caught when asked
to think what you want, not what I,
How Lopez limps up slow and shy
to say hello – how Pino never hesitates,
How this one here laughs quietly, abrazos out,
and that one cries at night
and we all hurt one time or more
and long to hear that drumming heart nearby.
The specks of dust quickscatter, die,
each one seen only once, and through a different sky.
It does occur to me that we
are all in love with people.

How shall I tell you?

after listening to the world news, the U.S.
attack on Libya, the Soviet accident at
Chernobyl, the firing of warships in the
Persian Gulf, and wondering . . . if . . .

When no soul walks the softened green
and no foot beats the pulse on crumbling brown
and no one lives to sing to rain
or soak to sun the spirit of its golden gown
to weave the many colors of the after-arch
from sky to human skin to wooded wealth
in fiber fabrics beads and tusks and seeds
all leading up in rows of beauty drumbeat to black
        neck, like venison in stealth

When no one lulls the child to sleep
or takes the wrinkled story's hand
or listens to the news – a wired sound
of tribe on tribe and – stet now – man on man
how shall I tell you that I love you then?
How shall I touch your fingers tip to tip
    and say that we were blood and human voice and friend?

Glossary:

(Note: Entries are alphabetized by the entire phrase as it occurs in the text, not by the most important word.)

Abrazar – to hug

Agua y cariñitos – water and affection

Allá también – over there too

Así, muy natural – like this, very natural

Así se acabó – so, it was done.

Aún – even

Aunque los que no están, molestan menos que este aquí – although the ones that aren't there bother me less than this one here

Bilingüe – bilingual

Cariños – affections

Chingas'as d'esas fregaderas. Ni me dejan tiempo de prender la vela – Screw those messes. They don't even leave me time to light the candle.

Como puede creer tal cosa – how can you believe such a thing

Compañía – company

Con mucho respeto – with lots of respect

Derecho, fuerte – straight, strong

Dios solo sabe – God only knows

Donde hay un lugar para tí – where there is a place for you

Es una tontería increíble – it's an incredible foolishness

Ese Vato – Pachuco slang for "That guy"

Está completamente equivocado – you are totally in error

Está usted loco – you are crazy

Estos Gringos con su – these gringos with their . . .

Familias grandes – big families

Hay un lugar – there is a place

Hielera – icebox

Hierbitas – herbs, plants

Jarros, ollas – pitchers, pots

Justicia! – justice!

Loquito – a bit crazy

Molcajete – a traditional Mexican mortar and pestle, used to
grind herbs and spices, made of volcanic stone

Mezcla – a mix

Nomás que – it's just that

No tienes límites – you have no limits

Pa' Juntarse – to get together

Para m'ija – to my daughter

Pedacito de la luna, Usted – piece of the moon, thou art

Pedacito de mi corazón – piece of my heart

Poquito aquí, poquito allá – a folk saying: "A little bit here,
a little bit there"

Por aquí , poquito – a little over here

Primos – cousins

Problemas de derechos humanos – human rights problems

Que se chingue Reagan – screw Reagan

Rebozo – a traditional Mexican shawl draped across
the shoulders

Rómpenles el borlote – tear up their scam

Sabor – flavor

Solito – all alone

Son así – (they) are like that

Vela – candle

Y a mí me gusta – and I like
Y el pobre – and the poor thing
Y las palabritas mías – and my little words
Y que pendejos porqué no – and why the hell not?
Y sus nietos – and their grandchildren
Y tráigame una cerveza – and bring me a beer
Ya Basta – enough!
Ya casi era tiempo de salir – it was almost time to leave
Ya ha comenza'o la revolución – the revolution's already
    begun

ABOUT THE AUTHOR

Called a "world class writer" by Alex Haley, Carmen Tafolla is widely recognized as one of the madrinas of contemporary Chicana literature. Born in San Antonio, Tafolla's poems employ the bilingual idiom of the city's westside barrios. She has long been regarded as one of the masters of bilingual code-switching in her fiction and poetry. *Curandera* (1983) is considered something of a core document in this regard. Tafolla is one of the most often anthologized Chicana writers in the country, and her dramatic talents have made her lively presentations highly sought after.

In the 1970s, Tafolla was the head writer for "Sonrisas," a pioneering bilingual television show for children. Many of Tafolla's stories for children have since been published as illustrated books by Scott Foresman, Houghton Mifflin, Celebration Press, and others. Her bilingual environmental story for children, *Baby Coyote and the Old Woman / El coyotito y la viejita*, was published by Wings Press in 2000.

A scholar of note, Tafolla is the author of *To Split a Human: Mitos, Machos y la Mujer Chicana* (1983). Tafolla received her Ph.D. in Bilingual Education from the University of Texas at Austin in 1982. She has been an Associate Professor and/or visiting professor of Women's Studies, Mexican American Studies, literature, and education at California State University Fresno, Northern Arizona University and other institutions throughout the Southwest. She has been a freelance educational consultant on bilingual education, writing and creativity, and cultural diversity issues for over two decades.

Tafolla is the author of *Sonnets to Human Beings and Other Selected Works*, which includes not only the title selection (recipient of the 1987 National Chicano Literature Prize from the University of California at Irvine), but a large selection of Tafolla's poems and short stories, as well as many essays on Tafolla and her work. Originally published in 1992 by Lalo Press and (in German) by the University of Osnabrück, *Sonnets to Human Beings and Other Selected Works* was reissued by McGraw-Hill in 1995 and (as a limited edition) by Wings Press in 1999.

Tafolla lives in San Antonio, Texas, where she is currently working on a novel, an autobiography, and a biographical work on labor leader Emma Tenayuca. She was a founder of Camino, an innovative dual-language school for gifted and creative students.

Colophon

This revised and expanded edition of *Sonnets and Salsa*, by Carmen Tafolla, has been entirely reset: The text has been set in a contemporary version of Classic Bodoni. The font was originally designed by 18th century Italian punchcutter and typographer, Giambattista Bodoni, press director for the Duke of Parma. Titles were set in Caslon Openface Type. *Sonnets and Salsa* has been printed on 70 pound paper containing fifty percent recycled fiber. All Wings Press books are designed and produced by Bryce Milligan.

Wings Press was founded in 1975 by Joanie Whitebird and Joseph F. Lomax as "an informal association of artists and cultural mythologists dedicated to the preservation of the literature of the nation of Texas." The publisher/editor since 1995, Bryce Milligan is honored to carry on and expand that mission to include the finest in American writing. To that end, we at Wings Press publish multicultural books, chapbooks, CDs and broadsides that enlighten the human spirit and enliven the mind. We know well that writing is a transformational art form capable of changing the world by allowing us to glimpse something of each other's souls.

Wings Press uses as much recycled material as possible, from the paper on which the books are printed to the boxes in which they are packed.

Other recent titles
from Wings Press

The Angel of Memory by Marjorie Agosín

Way of Whiteness by Wendy Barker

Hook & Bloodline by Chip Dameron

Incognito: Journey of a Secret Jew by María Espinosa

Peace in the Corazón by Victoria García-Zapata

Street of the Seven Angels by John Howard Griffin

Black Like Me by John Howard Griffin

Cande, te estoy llamando by Celeste Guzmán

Winter Poems from Eagle Pond by Donald Hall

Initiations in the Abyss by Jim Harter

Strong Box Heart by Sheila Sánchez Hatch

Patterns of Illusion by James Hoggard

With the Eyes of a Raptor by E. A. Mares

This Side of Skin by Deborah Paredez

Fishlight: A Dream of Childhood by Cecile Pineda

The Love Queen of the Amazon by Cecile Pineda

Bardo99 by Cecile Pineda

Face by Cecile Pineda

Smolt by Nicole Pollentier

Prayer Flag by Sudeep Sen

Distracted Geographies by Sudeep Sen

Garabato Poems by Virgil Suárez

Sonnets to Human Beings by Carmen Tafolla

Sonnets and Salsa by Carmen Tafolla

The Laughter of Doves by Frances Marie Treviño

Finding Peaches in the Desert by Pam Uschuk

One-Legged Dancer by Pam Uschuk

Vida by Alma Luz Villanueva

Wings Press Anthologies:

Cantos al Sexto Sol: A Collection of Aztlanahuac Writing
edited by Cecilio García-Camarillo, Roberto Rodríguez,
and Patrisia Gonzales

Jump-Start PlayWorks
edited by Sterling Houston

Falling from Grace in Texas:
A Literary Response to the Demise of Paradise
edited by Rick Bass and Paul Christensen

2005-2006 titles from Wings Press

Among the Angels of Memory / Entre los ángeles de la memoria
by Marjorie Agosín
The Scribbling Cure by Robert Bonazzi
Psst . . . I Have Something to Tell You, Mi Amor
by Ana Castillo
Drive by Lorna Dee Cervantes
Tropical Green by Chip Dameron
Tracking the Morning by Robert Fink
Burying the Farm by Robert Flynn
Wearing the River by James Hoggard
Inventing Emily: The True History of the Yellow Rose of Texas
by Denise McVea
Freize by Cecile Pineda
Indio Trails by Raúl Salinas
Songs Older Than Any Known Singer by John Phillip Santos
Scattered Risks by Pamela Uschuk

Our complete catalogue is available at
www.wingspress.com